Making Fabric Wall Hangings

Making Fabric Wall Hangings

Alice Timmins

B. T. Batsford Limited
Charles T. Branford Company

First published 1970
7134 2644 6
Branford SBN 8231 5024 0
Library of Congress Catalog Card Number 71 119561

Filmset by Keyspool Ltd, Golborne, Lancashire
Printed in Denmark by F. E. Bording Limited, Copenhagen
for the Publishers B. T. Batsford Limited, 4 Fitzhardinge Street,
London W.1 and Charles T. Branford Company, Newton Centre,
Massachusetts 02159

Contents

Acknowledgment

My thanks are due to all the artists who have allowed me to use illustrations of their work; to W. Bertheux (Curator, Department of Applied Art, Stedilijk Museum, Amsterdam), Anne Butler (Senior Lecturer and Head of Embroidery School, Faculty of Art and Design, Manchester Polytechnic), Corinne Campbell (Featherstone County Secondary Mixed School, Southall, Middlesex), Björn Hasselbad (Svenska Dagbladet, Stockholm), Bucky King (USA), Marie Spiby (Children's Reception Centre, Walton-le-dale, Lancashire) and Marjorie Timmins, for their cooperation; to Harry Timmins, who took most of the photographs; and to Catherine Timmins, who typed the manuscript.

Introduction

Fabric wall hangings and panels make interesting additions to any scheme of interior decoration; they add a welcome touch of individuality in an age when mass production is an inevitable part of life.

Fabric need not be regarded as merely a background for embroidery or any other form of decoration, though it will happily combine with many other materials. It has unique qualities which no other medium can provide, but these, as well as its limitations, must be understood and used sympathetically before anything of true value can be produced. An investigation into these qualities will reveal interesting possibilities to children and adults alike.

There is an immense range of fabrics of stimulating colours and textures available today, and many of the textiles woven from man-made fibres suggest treatments which would not have been possible before their invention. A spirit of adventure and willingness to experiment is of the highest importance, for without these the full possibilities of fabrics cannot be realised. Commercial 'kits' for fabric or felt picture making, for which nothing is needed except a limited amount of technical skill, cannot supply the same sense of achievement as original work based on personal vision. Children, especially, should be encouraged to create fabric pictures from their own impressions and observations—anything else limits their imagination and dulls their creative powers.

Fabrics provide not only a promising field of investigation for students at art colleges and colleges of education, but also a challenge to artists who work in other media. Research into the possibilities afforded by a different material may add much to their work.

Some of the many people who will have increased leisure because of automation may already have an interest in fabrics. For these, the making of panels or hangings could well prove a rewarding activity and could be the means of involving them more closely with their environment.

Working with fabrics can provide a valuable means of self-expression both in the designing and making of pictures or hangings, and also in the field of interior decoration. It is very satisfying to design a wall decoration which fits successfully into a particular scheme and which may indeed be the dominant feature of it.

This book presents ideas for using fabrics in various ways, but different individuals may find other methods which are more suited to their particular temperaments and skills. It shows how experiments will often give rise to fresh and original treatments which may prove to have interesting potentialities.

Plate 1
Fish Panel 860 mm × 300 mm (34 in. × 12 in.), by Marjorie Timmins. Small pieces of fabric are 'prodded' into polystyrene cut in the shape of a fish

Materials and tools

Fabrics

From the large number of varied types of fabrics woven from natural or man-made fibres, it should not be difficult to assemble a collection of many different colours, weights, textures and constructions. Dressmakers' scraps, 'fents' from market stalls, remnants of furnishing and dress fabrics can be acquired without much difficulty and all can be the means of achieving some special effect. It is worth while to buy small amounts of unusual fabrics when opportunity offers.

The following list will give some indication of the types of fabrics which may at some time be of use.

Heavy fabrics: tweeds, furnishing fabrics, velours
Lightweight and sheer fabrics: silks, nylons, cottons, curtain fabrics, net, lace
Shot and watered silks
Velvets
PVC
Hessian (burlap)
Fabrics containing lurex
Fur fabrics
Tape and ribbon
Fabrics created by knitting, crochet (1*a, b*) and darning or weaving
Printed fabrics should be used with discretion.

Other materials, such as glass, wood, leather, felt, metal, polythene, fur, polystyrene, beads, seeds, feathers, cords, buttons, sequins, nails, safety pins, washers and discarded materials may be used.

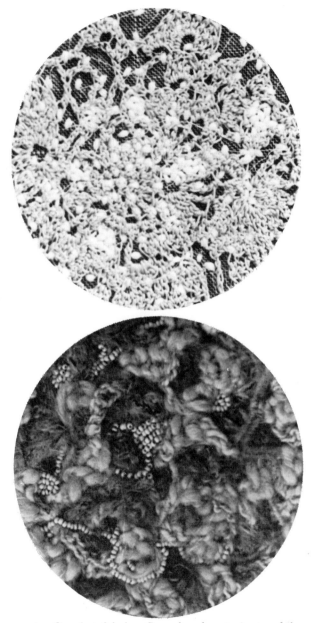

1*a, b* Crochet fabrics. Samplers by students of the Manchester Polytechnic, School of Embroidery

9

Threads

Various kinds, from very fine to very coarse, may be needed in any one panel.
Cotton: mercerised machine, embroidery, mending
Nylon and *Terylene*: invisible, machine, mending
Linen
Wool: knitting, rug, embroidery
Mohair
Chenille
Raffia
String and rope
Threads unravelled from fabrics
Lurex
Metallic threads

Needles

Sewing, crewel, chenille, tapestry, darning, bead.

Pins

Steel

Drawing pins (thumb tacks)

Staple gun

A useful item, if available

Scissors

Cutting out, embroidery

Thimble

Sewing machine

Not essential, but effective and time-saving. For some purposes a swing-needle type is useful, but the ordinary models are quite adequate in most cases.

Stretcher

Some panels need to be worked on a stretcher. Any machine stitching should, however, be done first. If the background fabric is rather fragile a backing of calico will be necessary, but firm thick fabrics will not need this. The fabric should be stretched smoothly and reasonably tightly, and fastened over to the back of the stretcher with staples or tacks, in the order shown in figure 2. A mark in the centre of each side of the fabric should be matched with ones on the centres of each side of the stretcher.

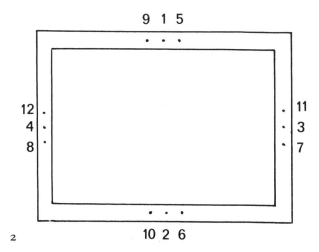

A stretcher for small panels can be made from four lengths of wood approximately 25 mm × 13 mm (1 in. × ½ in.) or 25 mm × 25 mm (1 in. × 1 in.), but thicker pieces are needed for large panels. These lengths should be first glued into place and then reinforced by panel pins (figure 3a). For large sizes, metal angles may be needed (figure 3b).

3a

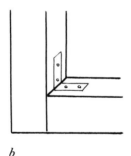

b

Adhesives
A latex adhesive, such as *Copydex* or *Evostick, Resin W*, which has a useful long nozzle on its container, is satisfactory for most purposes.

An impact adhesive may be needed for very heavy fabrics, and a transparent rubber solution, such as *Flameless* (used by milliners) is suitable for delicate ones.

Tambour frame
A round tambour frame is often useful for both machine and hand embroidery.

Backgrounds

Anything to which fabric can be attached, and which by some means can be hung up, will make a background for a wall hanging.
The following are the most suitable:

1 *Cardboard* or *paper* of any colour. It should be strong enough to hold fabric without tearing or buckling.

2 *Polystyrene* This is inexpensive and has possibilities for experiment. It should however be treated with care, as it is easily damaged. A cardboard backing or a frame will add strength.

3 *Softboard* This takes drawing pins easily.

4 *Wood* Off-cuts of various sizes can often be bought at low cost. As most wood is rather heavy for ordinary walls, the size may have to be restricted.

5 *Metal gauze* Fabrics may be sewn to this.

6 *Fabric*

7 *String* or *wire* fastened through a series of holes in a stretcher so as to form a kind of grid into which fabrics can be threaded or knotted.

8 *Chicken wire*

9 *Wood*

Ways of attaching fabric to background

Gluing to paper, cardboard (figure 4), polystyrene, wood. This is the easiest method for young children. If the panels are not intended to be permanent, a flour paste or cold water paste will be adequate. Latex adhesive is best for more permanent work and for polystyrene.

4 *Scrabster* by Marjorie Timmins. Fabrics glued on card with lines drawn with felt-tipped pen

Prodding This method can be used on polystyrene. Small pieces of fabric, 32 mm to 38 mm (1¼ in. to 1½ in.) square can be prodded into place with a suitable blunt-pointed tool such as a short knitting needle or large crochet hook or an old screwdriver with the corners rounded off (figure 5). A small dab of adhesive on the spot where the fabric is to go helps to hold it in place.

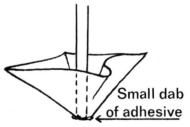

5 Method used for prodding

Any latex adhesive is suitable. Impact adhesives will be found to dissolve the polystyrene, but in some cases holes may be made deliberately as part of the design. The adhesive should be put on the polystyrene rather than on the fabric, and a dispenser with a long nozzle is ideal, especially for fixing down lengths of wool or string.

For this technique the polystyrene should be at least 19 mm ($\frac{3}{4}$ in.) thick, with a backing of strong cardboard. Thinner sheets are too fragile. See plate 1, facing page 8.

Drawing pins (thumb tacks) can be used to fasten fabrics to soft-board.

Sewing Shapes can be sewn to fabric by hand or machine stitching, using traditional appliqué methods and modern variations of them. The edges can be turned under or left as they are cut or torn.

All shapes should be tacked to the background or fixed with latex adhesive. This must be used very sparingly, as too much will cause a flat unfabric-like surface. Tackings can be removed if necessary when the shapes are finally sewn down.

Ways of sewing down the edges

1 The edges are frayed and sewn down with straight stitches in mercerised sewing cotton of a similar tone (6 and 7).

7

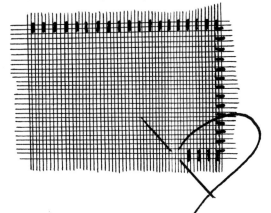

6

2 The edges are covered with long straight stitches. For this method the background must be held firmly in a frame (8). Herring bone, blanket stitch, running stitch, etc. could also be used.

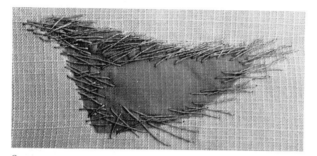

8

3 The edges of the shape are covered and held down by a couched boucle thread (9).

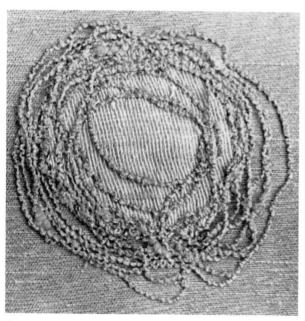

9

4 A circular shape is held down with many rows of machine stitching. Circular shapes sewn in this way, however, tend to pucker (10).

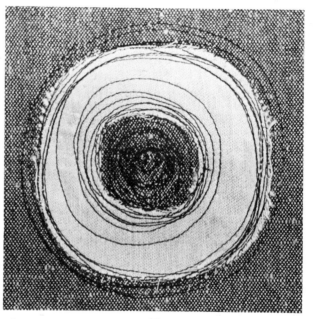

10

5 The tendency to pucker has been deliberately exploited. The centre has been padded with wool inserted through a small hole cut in the background fabric, afterwards sewn up (11).

6 Shapes can be sewn down with rows of machine stitching (12).

7 When several adjoining shapes are sewn down the machined lines can continue from one to the next and back again (13).

8 A zigzag stitch on a swing-needle machine will hold down raw edges adequately.

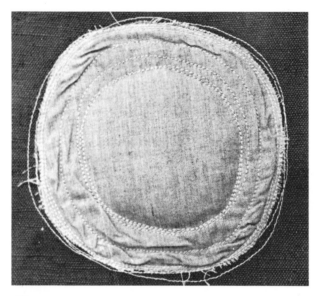

11

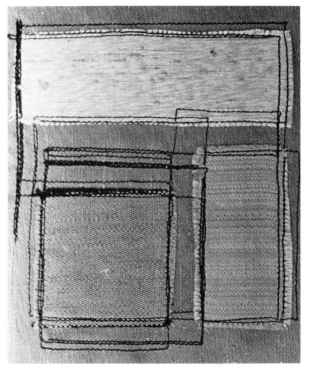

13

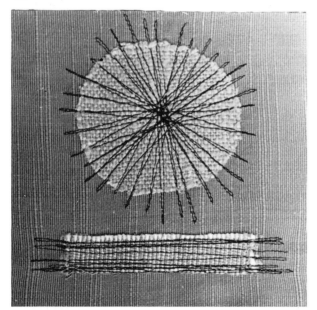

12

Turned edges

This method is suitable for uncomplicated shapes and gives a hard edge. On curved shapes the edges must first be snipped so that they will lie flat (14). A single turning is made over to the

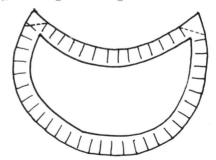

14

15

wrong side. The patch is then tacked and sewn to the background with invisible hemming (the needle being brought out exactly at the turning) or with ordinary hemming.

Another method is to tack or stitch the shape over firm card, *Vilene*, plywood or hardboard, and glue, or slipstitch it from the back near to the edge, on to the background (15).

Corners should be carefully treated, and surplus material cut away to reduce bulk.

15
Weaving
Small pieces of fabric can be created by weaving. A warp consiting of long straight stitches must

first be constructed on the background fabric and threads can be woven or darned through this (16).

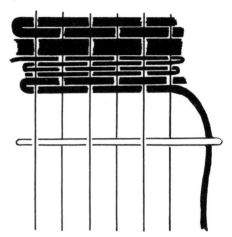

16

Fabric strips
Long thin strips of fabric (cut or torn) can be used for stitchery instead of embroidery threads if the background is of a loose weave. They can also be pulled through similar fabric using a crochet hook, leaving loops on the right side. This is the technique used for 'hooked' rugs (17).

Other rug techniques using spring or latchet hooks should be kept in mind for possible experiments.

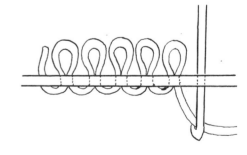

17

Approach to design

A rag-bag and a collection of odds and ends of varied materials in the classroom will provide opportunities for children to see, touch and talk about the different shapes, colours and textures. They should be encouraged to investigate the method of construction of fabrics by pulling them apart and by unravelling the threads, and they will then be able to relate their findings to experiences in weaving which they may have had. Children should be allowed to work spontaneously, each one discovering the methods best suited to his or her own abilities and temperament. The teacher should provide a stimulating atmosphere in which a spirit of enquiry and adventure may develop; and should be available for advice and help if needed.

The materials provided can be used in several ways to make pictures. It is useful to have some large strong envelopes or polythene bags in which to keep scraps of fabrics cut, torn or hacked off in early attempts to use scissors, together with bits of string, wool, raffia, wood (perhaps used matches or 'lolly' sticks), etc. Very small children will enjoy playing with these, and arranging them on a background of card, wood or fabric. They can be glued down or merely put back in the envelope or bag when the child has finished playing with them.

Older children may want to sew the materials to the fabric background. A piece of fabric, mounted on a stretcher or old picture frame, could be kept ready for any child who is ready to try experiments with needle and thread.

Fabrics can also be used on paper or card in place of, or combined with, paint, or to add colour to a charcoal or felt pen drawing. On the other hand, the fabrics can be the starting point,

Plate 2
From Klara to Marieberg   Fabric panel 3 m × 6 m (10 ft × 20 ft), by Ulla Grytt. In the entrance hall of the offices of the newspaper Svenska Dagbladet, Stockholm. Lettering is newsprint on fabric

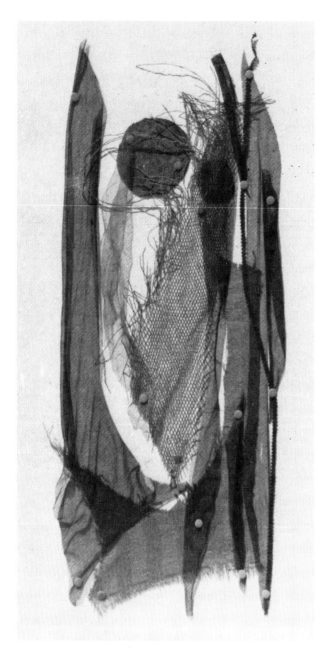

and the drawing or painting made over them after they have been glued down on paper or card.

Another useful background material which can be kept in a classroom is a piece of softboard. Fabric shapes can be cut out and moved around until the arrangement satisfies the child. They can then be held down with drawing pins (thumb tacks), which will form part of the design (18). The softboard can be used again and again.

Offcuts of wood can often be acquired at a low cost. Young children enjoy hammering in nails so as to hold down the pieces of fabric; in fact the picture making may prove to be a secondary consideration.

Polystyrene is also an inexpensive material to use as a background and, if framed, is quite durable.

Experiments using materials such as metal gauze, chicken wire, rug canvas, etc., will all help to increase understanding of and respect for materials.

18 Fabric fastened with drawing pins (thumb tacks) to softboard

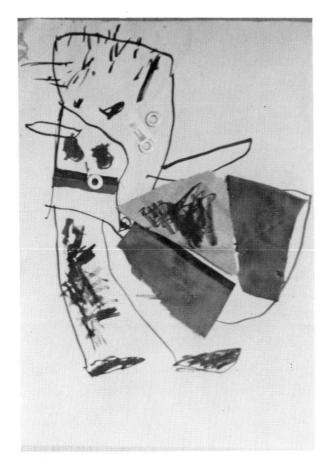

19 *Soldier Drummer* by Oliver, aged 4 years

20 *Soldier* by Mark, aged 6 years. Fabric and felt-tipped pen drawing on paper. 'Medals' are stocking label, washer, and part of cigarette packet

21   Fabrics and wool nailed to chipboard by Mark, aged 6 years

22   Panel by Mandy, aged 7 years, who was taken into care by the Children's Department of the Lancashire County Council, suffering from the effects of physical and mental cruelty. This was the first piece of work in which she was able to take any interest after several weeks in care

23–4   Panels by pupils at Featherstone County
Secondary Mixed School, Southall, Middlesex

23   *Butterfly* by Jasbir Chana

24 *Fictitious Animal* by Sheila Shepherd

25 *Sun and flowers* by Margery, aged 9 years

Design

A design for a fabric wall hanging generally has its origin in an impression received through one of the senses and which arouses some emotion.

The colours, shapes and textures of everyday objects and their relation to each other may be a source of inspiration, and a collection of shells, rocks, stones and 'waste' objects can often give ideas.

Unusual natural phenomena, events such as a funeral, a fête or a football match, the behaviour of animals or insects, television programmes, and man-made objects of innumerable kinds, can each suggest a starting point. The sight of a piece of fabric of unusual colour, texture or construction may give rise to a desire to experiment with ways of using it.

In fact, subjects for pictures are everywhere, and though some people have a natural capacity to see them, others need to educate themselves to do so. It is necessary to look closely and sensitively at our surroundings, and to see things not superficially, but with perception; to see not only the shape, colour and texture, but to search for the underlying qualities such as grace, power, beauty, determination, fear, and even brutality and ugliness. A picture is not necessarily pretty or pleasant to look at (a crucifixion, for example).

A sketch book is of immense value, but for those who have no confidence in their ability to draw, records and experiments can be made using paper, fabric, string, etc., and photographs and pictures cut from magazines and periodicals may form a useful supplement. Visits to art galleries, museums and exhibitions will provide stimulation and a field for study.

Once the subject has presented itself, many other things will affect it consciously or unconsciously; personal reactions, imagination and capacity for fantasy, the ability to recognise important aspects and to reject others, awareness of contemporary life, a recognition of the qualities seen in the work of artists using other media, tradition, and the possibilities and limitations of the materials and techniques used.

Intuition, too, has an important part to play, as its suppression will cause work to lack significance and vitality. It is intuition which gives individual style and character to an artist's work and which, metaphorically speaking, stamps it with his or her own signature.

However realistic a representation of a scene or object may appear to be, generally some adaptation, simplification, distortion or re-arrangement of shapes and colours will have taken place to conform with the requirements of fabrics and technique and to achieve an expressive composition.

When some aspect of the character of a subject (eg, weight, sadness) or some part of it (eg, a mouth) is selected and interpreted in terms of colour, texture, movement, etc, an 'abstract' results.

Some fabric panels are entirely non-representational and purely decorative. Such results can be achieved when the designs are made by experimenting with ways of cutting and arranging shapes, making ink spots, doodling, printing, throwing down pieces of fabric in a random arrangement, or by experimenting in ways of using unusual fabrics.

In addition to this, a good design must show awareness of all the following aspects, not necessarily in this order:

Lines and shapes; Colour
Texture and decoration
Technique; Purpose.

26

Lines

The lines in a fabric picture may sometimes be drawn, but are often made with threads, and there is such diversity in the types available that there should be little difficulty in finding the ones which are best suited to each particular purpose.

A line is also formed where two pieces of fabric of different tones lie alongside and touch each other or overlap, and this should be related to other lines in the composition.

Lines can be thick or thin, horizontal, vertical, diagonal or curved (26); their position and character can in many circumstances help to emphasise movement and interpret emotions. They can appear to change position and direction in certain situations and this can cause optical illusions which can be used in a composition (27).

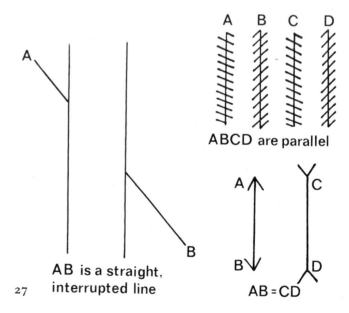

A   B   C   D

ABCD are parallel

AB = CD

27 AB is a straight, interrupted line

It is not always necessary to make a completely unbroken line; the energy in it will make it appear to continue its direction (28).

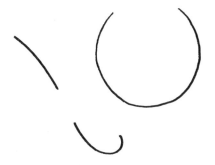

28

Shapes

A conscious effort to see the shapes with which we are surrounded will in time become an unconscious habit. A record, *with details ignored,* should be made by sketching (or cutting out in paper) shapes of special interest. These should include rocks, stones, shells, vegetables, fruit, flowers, trees, and shapes seen in snow and on sand, mud or water.

Man-made environments such as cities with towering buildings, complexes of roads and railways, traffic and interesting sky-lines; docks, with cranes, ships and piles of goods, power stations, factories, shops and scrap yards all have a wealth of interesting shapes.

Minute objects seen through a microscope show unexpected forms in details invisible to the naked eye. Photomicrographs are available which show some fantastic and beautiful shapes.

Fresh aspects of everyday objects can be found by looking at them from unusual viewpoints: 'worm's eye' and 'bird's eye' views of things are very different.

Not only should the shapes themselves be recorded, but also the 'negative' shapes, ie the shapes formed between objects grouped together. In a picture these are just as important as the shapes themselves. The branches of a tree often enclose a number of interesting 'negative' shapes, and the spaces between chimneys, groups of houses, the leaves of plants or a pile of onions are worth recording.

The following are some ways in which many different shapes can be made by cutting or tearing pieces from squares, circles or triangles. Most of these can be related in some way to everyday objects. Square and rectangular shapes suggest houses and buildings, circles and oblongs suggest stones, fruits, vegetables, or clouds, and triangles suggest tents, mountains, etc.

It is better to use only black and white at first; colour should be introduced in similar exercises later.

1 Start with several black squares and cut or tear off curves from the corners making various 'carresque' shapes (29).

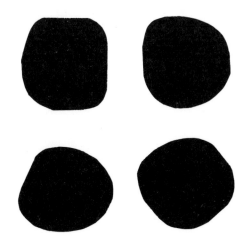

29

25

2 Cut out pieces from circles (30), rectangles (31), squares (32) and triangles (33).

30

31

32

33

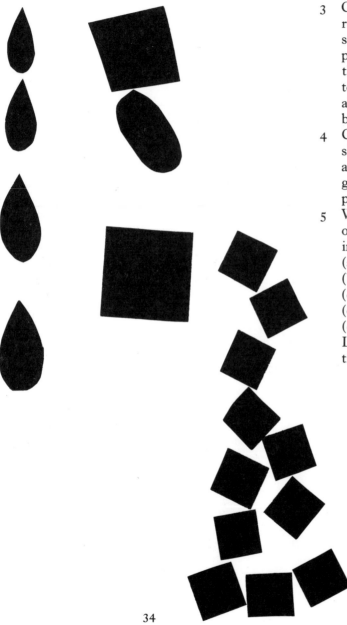

3 Cut out a number of small narrow black rectangles. Arrange these to show a crowd scene such as an accident, an open air political meeting or a procession, emphasizing the focal point by isolating it or by adding a touch of strong bright colour. This could also be done with used matches, on a darker background.

4 Choose one shape and cut several more of similar shape but of different sizes and arrange them on a plain or patterned background. (Newspaper or printed patterned paper could be used.)

5 With any of these shapes, cutting or tearing others if needed, make arrangements showing:

(a) pressure   (f) release
(b) collapse   (g) peace
(c) flight   (h) conflict
(d) speed   (i) growth
(e) imprisonment   (j) excitement

Lines could be added if necessary. (Illustration 34 suggests 'falling'.)

34

6 Cut up a square of black paper into smaller pieces of varying sizes and re-arrange them (35a, b and c).

7 Repeat this with a circle, an oval, or any other shape.

35a

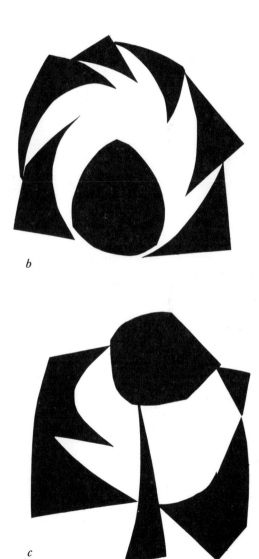

b

c

8 Cut out one or two simple shapes in different sizes and move them around until the arrangement seems pleasing (36).

9 Shapes can be 'extended' by cutting them up and moving the pieces away from each other (37a–e).

When placing the shapes on a background it may be found that the scale is not satisfactory. The shapes may be too small, causing them to look insignificant, or too large, causing crowding. If so, a smaller or larger piece of paper should be used for the background.

The next step is to create compositions in the same ways but with coloured paper (pages from magazines), tissue, metallic, corrugated and textured papers, as well as fabrics, threads and drawn lines.

36

37a

b

c

d

e

Colour

People who have been given the opportunity to involve themselves with colour in everyday activities in their early years are more likely to use it with discrimination and appreciation as they grow older.

Young children use colour with great confidence in exciting and often unexpected combinations. They need little help in making fabric pictures apart from the provision of materials; chiefly a wide range of fabrics of as many hues as possible, from which they must be allowed to make their own choice. Some have a preference for pale colours, while others will select sombre or flamboyant ones; their choice is a natural expression of personality.

They should be encouraged to look at, and talk about, the colours they see around them.

Many adults have prejudices about colour due to early influences, fashion, past experiences or associations and sometimes to superstition, and these may prevent them from using colour in an uninhibited way. The chief barrier to its effective use is, however, a lack of training in actually *seeing* the colours which surround them. The idea that a leaf is green, a tree trunk brown, and the sky blue, is only part of the truth.

Exercises such as the following may help towards a wider appreciation of the characteristics and behaviour of colour. If recorded and kept in a file or sketch book they would be useful as a reference. Paints, crayons or coloured paper could, where appropriate, supplement the use of fabrics.

A pile of scraps of as many colours as possible should be spread out and moved about, as sometimes accidental juxtapositions of colours will give inspiration.

1 Pick out a piece of fabric which attracts by its colour, and make a list of things it brings to mind—man-made, natural, or abstract qualities. Repeat with other colours.

2 Select two or three different sets of colours which make an attractive scheme and stick scraps in a sketch book.

3 Repeat this with colours which seem repellant. Some of these may be seen to have unusual and exciting possibilities.
In both 2 and 3 find the proportions of the colours which seem to be most effective.

4. Collect as many different greens as possible and stick down a scrap of each in a sketch book. Repeat with other colours—reds, browns, blues, etc.

5 Note the effect of atmosphere or artificial lighting effects on colour. Analyse the colours of, for example, a building on a sunny day, on a dull day, after a fall of snow or with floodlighting. Match these in fabrics.

6 Make an analysis of the colours seen in any object such as a vegetable, fruit or flower. The shape and proportions of the colours should be approximately shown, but no attempt at an accurate pictorial rendering should be made.

7 Find sets of colours which express some emotion—sorrow, joy, temper, etc.

8 Select colours which suggest heat and others which suggest coldness.

9 Find pieces of fabric of hues which seem to interpret the spirit of a particular poem or piece of music.

Plate 3
Teenagers Detail of co-operative work by students training as house-mothers at the training centre in Kirkham, Lancashire. The average age was 19 years and most of these students had a limited experience of art and needlecraft

Experiments in colour theory

These experiments can best be carried out with fabrics of the three primary hues (red, yellow and blue), in their purest form. The fabrics should be smooth (eg, cotton poplin). In addition, transparent fabrics (eg, net or nylon chiffon) in the same hues and in black and white will be needed, together with the rest of a fabric collection. In some cases, paints, crayons or coloured paper could be used.

Colour has three characteristics or dimensions which work together to form the colour content of a wall-hanging.

Hue: it is red, violet, yellow, brown, etc.

Tone: it is dark or light.

Intensity: is its colour content or amount of saturation. Colours of the spectrum are of maximum intensity.

Primary colours

Cut small pieces of the three primary hues, red, blue and yellow.

Secondary colours

Cut similar pieces of the same colours in transparent fabrics. Place transparent yellow over blue fabric, making green, transparent blue over red, making violet, and transparent red over yellow, making orange.

Complementary or contrasting colours

Each possible hue has its contrasting or complementary colour, and when they are placed together, each seems to increase in vividness and vitality, to the point of quarrelling. Find the colours in a pile of fabrics which seem to react to each other in this way.

Construct illustration 38 with the colours

indicated. Stare at the black spot in a good light (preferably strong daylight) and look at a clear white surface. An after-image of each square in its complementary colour will appear.

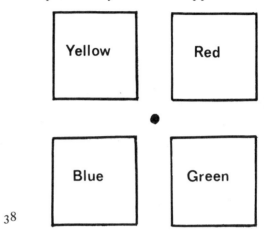

38

Tints and tones

Place transparent white squares over squares of any colour. These colours will then appear to be paler, and are called tints of the original colour.

Repeat this using black transparent fabric instead of white. The darker hues which result are called tones.

Many tints and tones of any colour of the spectrum and of mixtures of them are available in fabrics.

Colour mixing

Subtle shades of brown, grey, khaki, olive green, etc, should be included in a fabric collection. Try to match these by placing transparent fabrics over opaque ones or by using several layers of transparent fabrics, or by mixing in paints varying amounts of the primary colours, with the addition of black, grey or white if necessary.

Tone

The lightness or darkness of a hue is called its tone, and beginners often ignore the fact that this is an important part of the colour content of a picture.

A look at a collection of fabrics will show that some colours are naturally lighter in tone than others. Yellow seems to be the lightest, then orange and yellow green, red and green rather darker, then blue and violet deepest of all.

Besides this, any tone of a colour is darker than, and any tint is lighter than the colour itself.

Tone values are easier to distinguish if the eyes are half-closed or if they are seen in a dim light.

Exercises

1 Take small pieces of all the different grey fabrics available and arrange them in a column, starting with a white piece and placing the greys in order of tone until the darkest is reached. Finish with a black piece (39).

2 Arrange all the greens in a similar way.

3 Repeat with pinks and reds.

4 Repeat with greens.

5 Repeat with blues.

6 Repeat with browns.

7 Arrange some pieces of fabrics of *different* colours and tones in the same way.

8 Take a number of pieces of different colours but of the same tone and place them in a group, touching or overlapping. Then cut a piece of fabric of the same shape and tone as the finished group and put this nearby. Which is the more interesting?

39 White, greys and black showing graduation of tone

Behaviour of colour

Colour is an active, not a passive thing, and the

reactions of colours to each other in certain situations can make them appear to change in hue, size, temperature, tone and mood; and so affect their use in a picture.

Hue
Take three identical squares of grey fabric (dyed, not constructed with black warp and white weft). Place them on large squares of red, blue and yellow, and note how the coloured squares seem to absorb some of their own hue from the grey squares. (Grey is a mixture of blue, red and yellow.)

Size
Cut out two yellow squares of about 50 mm (2 in.) and place one on a larger white square and one on black. Look at them at a distance of about 1830 mm (2 yards), and note how the yellow on white appears to move forward and increase in size. Try blue on white and on black and note the difference.

Temperature
Place one of the yellow squares on a larger orange (warm colour) and the other on a blue–green (cold) background. Note how the blue–green field makes the yellow look hotter (moving to orange).

Tone
Place one yellow square on its complementary (violet) and the other on its neighbouring one (orange). Note how the one on the violet field appears to be lighter.

Mood
In the same arrangement, note how the yellow square on the orange field seems calm and peaceful, and on violet it appears violent and aggressive.

Find sets of colours which work together agreeably, and others which react to each other in an aggressive way.

Texture

Textures are particularly varied in fabrics and they can be both seen and felt. Contrasting rough and smooth ones create surface interest in a wall hanging; their different qualities being emphasised by their juxtaposition. A rough tweed for example will look rougher, and a satin smoother, if they are placed together.

Not only contrasts in the textures themselves, but contrasts in the size of the rough and smooth areas should be considered, as equal proportions could look monotonous.

An interesting experiment would be to collect different textures of one colour and use them in a design, exploiting the effect of the textural variations on the colour.

Fabric textures may suggest qualities such as:
The delicacy of a flower.
The rigidity of metal.
The hardness of stone.
The flamboyance of pomp.
The slipperiness of a fish.
The roughness of a tree trunk.

An attempt should be made to assess the particular qualities of the materials which are handled or seen.

Decoration

This must be considered at the same time as texture, as it is often the means of creating textural interest in some particular area.

No decoration at all may be needed on a wall hanging, as the fabrics and the way they are used may be interesting enough in themselves. Sometimes, however, small elaborately treated areas may have a dramatic effect, and in other cases the whole or most of the surface may be heavily encrusted.

The indiscriminate scattering of bits of decoration, particularly if they are unrelated to each other, should be avoided, and it must be realised that no amount of elaboration will conceal poor design.

In wall hangings, decoration often takes the form of embroidery, by hand, machine, or both, but many other materials such as wood, fur, metal, beads, nails, plastics or found or discarded objects may be what is needed to convey a particular impression. In their natural context (fur for an animal) they may look uninteresting and even ridiculous, but placed in unexpected surroundings they may be amusing or have an element of shock or be transformed in an exciting way. Enrico Baj wittily uses a thermometer for a nose in 'Lady sensitive to the weather'.

Technique

Technique should be regarded as a means to an end, not as an end in itself. It should be neither over-careful or careless, but carefree, unselfconscious and no more than adequate, and this involves an understanding of, and sympathy with, tools and materials.

In experimental work, some techniques will obviously have to be invented or adapted.

Traditional embroidery stitches may be used in a much freer way on wall-hangings than on domestic articles, as long stitches, which might easily be caught and pulled on a cushion or table linen, will be free from this risk when hanging on a wall.

Sympathetic use of materials

Each type of fabric has its own individual character; smoothness, roughness, softness, harshness, springiness, limpness, slipperiness, flimsiness, delicacy or sturdiness. It can be dull or shiny, woven with fine, thick or nobbly threads or with a mixture of them all. It can be opaque or transparent, or can have a shot or watered effect, and a sympathetic use of a particular type of fabric is part of a good technique.

All fabrics can be cut, and some can be torn, leaving an interesting edge. Some fabrics have warp and weft of different colours, and unravelled edges of these reveal lines which can give interest to a colour scheme.

In some loosely woven types, threads can be moved about, leaving gaps. Drawing out threads produces a somewhat similar effect.

Fabrics can be folded, rolled, puckered, stretched and padded. Interesting effects can be achieved by superimposing transparent fabrics on themselves or on opaque ones.

Unravelled threads or narrow strips of fabric can be used for embroidery or to create pieces of knitting, crochet, darning or weaving which can form part of a design.

The character of fabric should never be disguised—a fabric picture should be unmistakably recognisable as such. It is no recommendation to say that it is just like a painting or an etching.

Tools

The tools which are needed should be kept in good condition: the sewing machine oiled, needles unrusted and straight, and scissors sharp.

The needles should be suited to the thread and fabric and should not be so coarse that they will damage either of them. The eyes should be large enough to allow for easy threading.

A great deal of experimental work can be done with the sewing machine. Different threads in the spool and alterations of tension will create different effects. Time spent in finding out what the machine will do will not be wasted.

A round tambour frame should be used with care, as the rings may leave pressure marks on delicate fabrics or on stitchery already done. Tape or a strip of soft fabric wound round the inner ring will give some protection.

When the handling of materials and tools is fully understood and practised so that it becomes almost effortless, sensible and effective techniques will more easily be found.

Suitability for purpose

If a panel is to be designed for a particular room, all the existing features should be taken into account; size, amount of wall space available, type of furniture, colour of curtains and carpet or rugs, existing pattern if any, and the position of doors, windows and furniture. Colours which can be seen through an open door may also need to be considered.

A small panel may look insignificant in a large room containing little furniture, but on the other hand a large panel if not of strongly contrasting colours and tones may look pleasing in a small room.

The shape and size of the panel should be decided first. A short wide panel will appear to decrease the height of a room with a high ceiling, while a long narrow one will have the opposite effect. A large panel of advancing colours and strong tonal contrasts will decrease the apparent distance of a wall from the viewer, so making

40   Lancashire Industrial scene

37

41 Shapes of industry—533 mm × 1953 mm (21 in. × 77 in.)

the room appear to be smaller, while retreating colours and less strong tonal contrasts will make a wall appear to recede.

The panel should be placed so as to make an interesting combination of shapes when placed in relation to the furniture, doors and windows.

The colours in the panel can be used to make a room look colder or warmer, so that in a room facing north, yellows and oranges and reds will create an effect of sunshine, while a sunny room may need cool blues and greens. If these colours are already used for carpet or curtains, however, a contrast may be introduced by means of the panel.

If there are already interesting shapes in a patterned carpet or curtains, these shapes, not necessarily of the same size, or exactly the same shape, could be the basis of the design for the fabric picture.

42 Panel 41 shown in context of a room

43   Arms of the City of London. Panel 1220 mm ×
915 mm (4 ft × 3 ft) by Pat Russell and Elizabeth
Ward

Composition

Shapes and lines, colours and textures should be arranged in a fabric picture so as to lead the eye in a kind of voyage of exploration, moving quickly or directly or meandering slowly; being induced to stop at interesting places, exploring them and discovering relationships or contrasts between them and returning by different routes to these centres of interest.

The general direction of these movements may be chiefly circular, triangular, horizontal, vertical, radiating or exploding from a point, or diagonal, and this helps to emphasise the mood.

In representational pictures there is often one main centre of interest, and this is generally not placed exactly in a central position.

Many different ways of composing a picture are shown in this book. Some are symmetrical, some almost so, many are not. A study of the various ways in which important features are placed and emphasised should prove to be of value.

44 *At Midsummer Time* by Lea Thil-Junnila of Helsinki, using rya rug technique

Making a start

There is no single way of setting out to make a fabric panel. When the nature of some particular piece of fabric is the point of departure, experiments in its use may suggest a subject and a way to begin.

Some adults with a background of trained observation, sketching and experimental work, prefer to make a start without any preliminary drawing, but with a more or less clear idea of what they want the result to be. They will experiment and adapt as they go on.

Others prefer to make a drawing first, but this should not be strictly followed, as modifications will be necessary so as to solve problems which may arise and to use successfully any discoveries which they may make about the fabrics used. To trace a complete set of outlines on the fabric and to follow them faithfully is likely to produce a result which lacks spontaneity and vitality.

The only time when an accurate drawing must be made and used is in the type of patchwork illustrated on plate 5, facing page 57.

The subject of the panel having been decided upon, thought should be given to the fabrics which will be most suited to its character, and to the technique which will suit the statement to be made.

The type of background should first be selected. If it is to be of fabric, it can either be one large piece (backed if necessary) or made of patchwork. In this case, the pieces may be seamed together first, or they may be placed, with edges overlapping, so as to cover completely a piece of calico of the required size, and sewn down in whatever way seems appropriate.

The area of the finished work should be marked, leaving a border of several inches all round, as the design may need more room. A lining may be needed, especially if machining is to be done.

Any shapes should be cut out, prepared if necessary (see pages 12–16) and pinned in place. Added lines may be indicated with threads, also pinned down.

It is wise then to hang up the panel for a few days, looking at it occasionally at the distance at which it will probably been seen. It should be looked at both in full and in half light, so that any alterations to shapes, lines, colours, tones and textures may be made.

If machining is to be done, this is the time to do it. When the work is not to be put on a stretcher, it should be pressed on the wrong side on a thick soft pad, using a steam iron or a damp cloth, so as to eliminate any puckering which may have occurred. Great care should be taken, and a small piece of the background fabric tested first, if possible. If the panel is to be put on a stretcher, no ironing will be needed.

Any additional work should then be done, but it is wise to review the situation at intervals, so as to avoid unnecessary or incongruous additions.

Various ways of finishing and mounting are described in the following section.

Overleaf
45 *Vermilion on Cobalt Blue*, 686 mm × 406 mm (27 in. × 16 in.). A panel involving the drawing out of some threads and their use, together with some embroidery cottons, for darning into the threads left. Some groups of threads are manipulated so as to form patterns, and sewn down. Note method of hanging

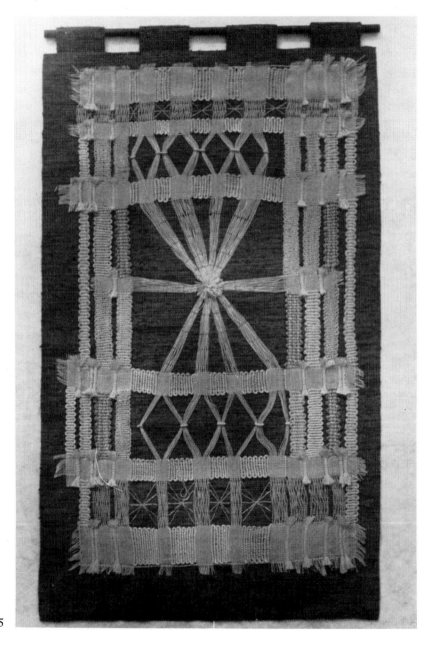

45

Finishing

In the method of hanging, the character of the panel must be kept in mind.

Most panels need to be hung simply as a square, rectangle, circle, or whatever shape the design demands. The way of hanging them up should not be visible.

In some cases, however, a more elaborate effect may be needed to carry out the theme (see figure 45) and some ways may have to be invented as in figure 90.

Fabric panels which are worked or mounted on a stretcher can be framed with strips of wood or metal, preferably mitred at the corners. The wood may be painted, or left in its natural state.

Small panels can be stretched over a piece of strong card. Mounting board is better than strawboard which may eventually discolour the fabric. The edges must be turned over to the back, and glued down or laced from side to side. The corners should be mitred (figure 46). The panels can then be framed or glued down on a larger piece of hardboard or mounting board.

Another simple way of finishing is to stretch the panel over a piece of hardboard, gluing it to the edges only, and cutting off surplus material at the back. The edges can then be finished with a strip of folded fabric, tape or braid (figure 47).

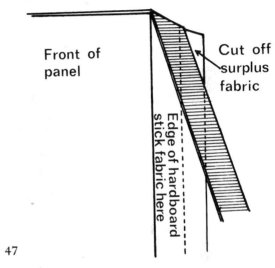

Front of panel

Cut off surplus fabric

Edge of hardboard stick fabric here

47

Some panels, however, are free-hanging, and though great care and precision is needed to ensure that they hang well, they do retain most completely the character of the fabrics.

They must first of all be prepared for mounting. If there is no embroidery or other decoration, they can be gently but firmly stretched and pressed under a damp cloth or with a steam iron. Otherwise they should be placed face upward on a board (or a wooden floor) covered with damp blotting paper and held down and stretched into shape with drawing pins (thumb tacks) placed closely together round the edges. When completely dry they are ready to be made up in the following way (figure 48):

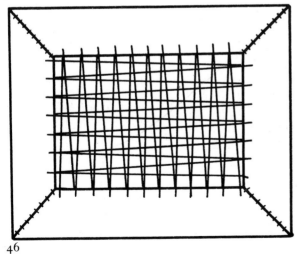

46

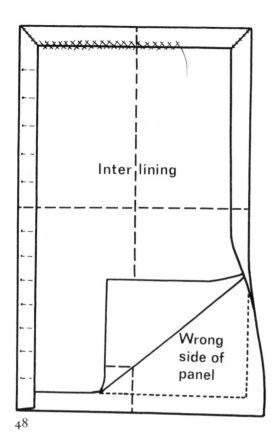

Inter|lining

Wrong
side of
panel

48

49

50

1 Cut an interlining of heavyweight *Vilene* or strong firmly woven fabric of the exact size that the finished panel is to be, making sure that each corner is a right angle and that the sides are perfectly straight.

2 Tack a centre line vertically and horizontally on both panel and interlining.

3 Place the panel face down on a flat surface with the interlining on top, matching the tackings.

4 Turn and pin down the surplus fabric over the edges of the interlining, and catch it down with herringbone stitch, making sure that no stitches show on the right side of the panel.

5 Slipstitch a backing of lining fabric reaching to about 6 mm ($\frac{1}{4}$ in.) from each edge.

Hanging

1 For a large heavy wall-hanging, a batten plugged into the wall may be necessary. Curtain rings sewn at intervals of about 152 mm (6 in.) at the top of the hanging can then be passed over small hooks or nails at the top of the batten.

2 Another way is to pass the rings through a length of dowel and to hang this over a hook in the wall (figure 49).

3 Still another method is to pass a strip of wood (about 25 mm × 13 mm (1 in. × $\frac{1}{2}$ in.) section) between the front of the panel and its lining at both top and bottom. This should not interfere with the flat surface of the panel, so extra material must be allowed in the lining to accommodate it (figure 50). The lining is nailed to the piece of wood at the top with 10 mm ($\frac{3}{8}$ in) tin tacks at 102 mm

(4 in.) intervals. A long nail with a large head, or square hook (two for a big panel), should be plugged into the wall, and a small hole made in the lining just below the strip of wood. The nail, or hook, is pushed through this hole and under the wood (figure 51).

4 Strips of wood or metal (such as brass pelmet strip obtainable at most hardware shops and some chain stores), sometimes make a satisfactory finish. Victorian brass stair rods are of a suitable length for some panels.

The wood is stapled or fastened with tacks or drawing pins (thumb tacks) over the top and bottom edges of the panel. This is a simple method which children can use.

In the case of metal strip, holes may be drilled at intervals and the metal polished and coated with clear varnish before it is sewn to the top and bottom of the panel with stitches through the holes.

These panels are hung by means of a cord or a ring at the middle of the top strip.

5 Some panels may need a more elaborate way of hanging which will enhance the design (page 42). The required number of squares of the same materials as the background are folded as in figure 52a (making three thicknesses) and the centre folded edges are slipstitched together. The resulting rectangles are then doubled and sewn to the top of the panel at the back, one edge slightly above the other so as to avoid bulk (figure 52b). The lining is then sewn on.

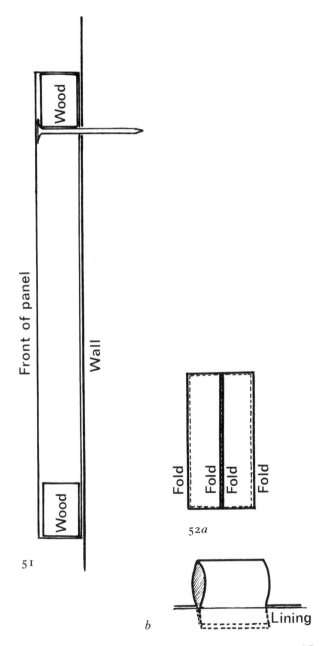

Front of panel

Wood

Wall

Wood

51

Fold   Fold   Fold   Fold

52a

b

Lining

Fabrics on polystyrene

Polystyrene tiles should be backed with strong card, or framed in some way. Latex adhesive should be used.

Opposite
53 *Gossips,* 300 mm (12 in. square). This panel is made from strips of black lace, braid, silk, wool, and nets of various types, stuck to a polystyrene tile. The sun is cut from gold kid

Overleaf
54 *Grid,* 300 mm (12 in. square). The basis of this design is a grid made of threads unravelled from a grey furnishing fabric. The circles are chenille, un- ravelled from the border of the same piece of material, from which are also cut some of the squares. Various blues, greens and browns with some knitted gold lurex are used for the rest of the squares

53

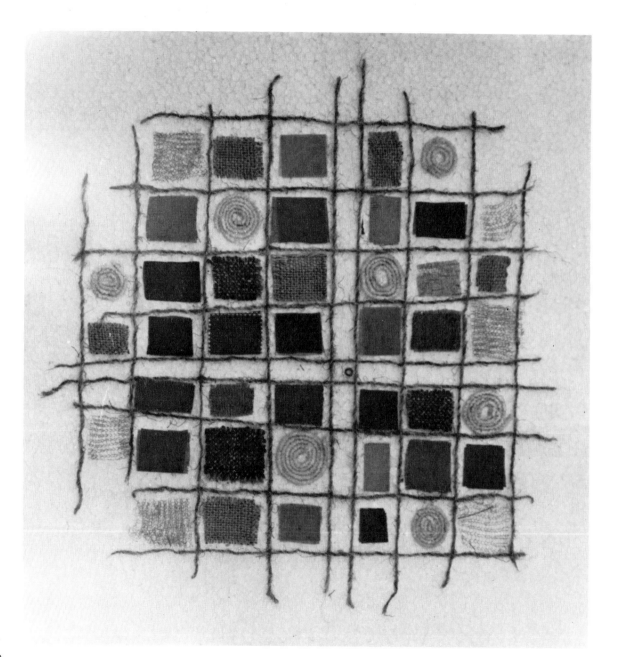

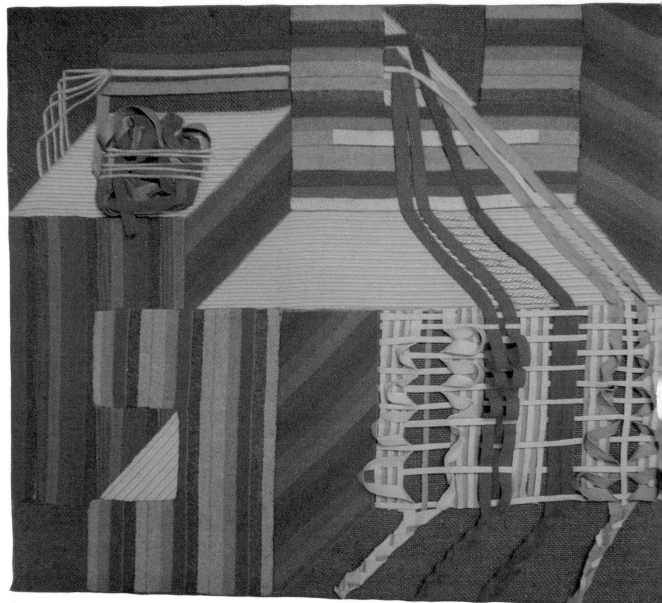

Plate 4
Platform by Christine Hunt, first year student,
Manchester   Polytechnic, School of Embroidery

Samplers

55a, b Sheer fabric treated in various ways by Jane
Arand, second year student at Manchester Polytechnic, School of Embroidery

56 Threads in polythene with machine stitching by Lynn Mulhall, second year student at Manchester Polytechnic, School of Embroidery

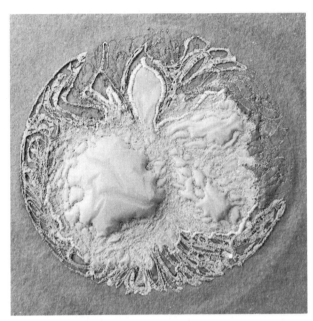

57 PVC padded and sewn down by machine by Lynn Mulhall, second year student at Manchester Polytechnic, School of Embroidery

58 Sampler showing experiments with threads, fabrics and leather by first year student at Manchester Polytechnic, School of Embroidery

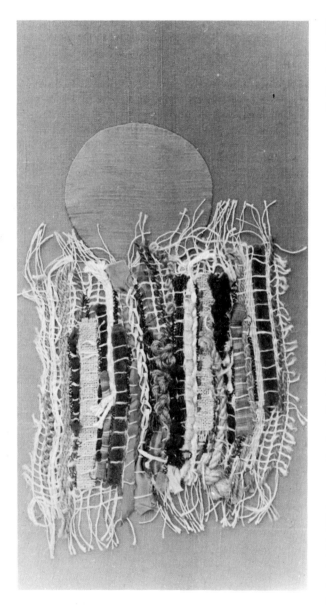

Experiments in making and using fabrics

The starting point for these three panels was a small piece of very coarsely woven cream curtain fabric.

Harvest (figure 59)   Narrow strips of silk, linen, PVC, nylon stocking, velvet and hessian were darned into the smaller piece, together with string, rope, rug wool and embroidery threads. In colour these were natural to brown with touches of bright red, darker red, orange and magenta.

Moon Flower (figure 60)   The fabric was cut into two pieces, the larger of which was bleached. Most of the threads were drawn out leaving a long stem with a few threads crossing it at the top. These were curved upwards round a circle of coarse white linen (over heavyweight *Vilene*) giving a hard edge as a contrast to the wavering character of the threads. The background is of dark grey and black furnishing fabric.

59   *Harvest*

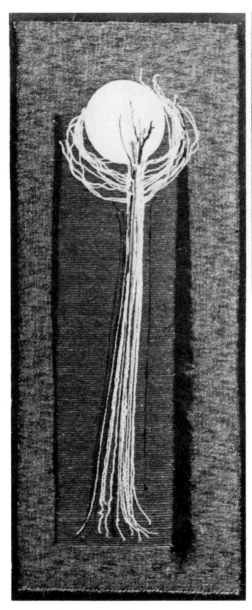

60 *Moon Flower*

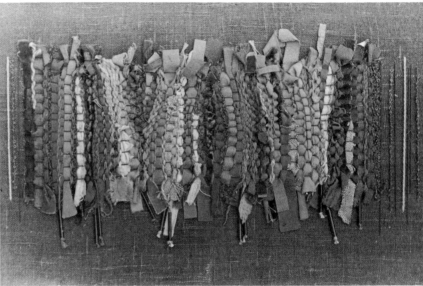

61 *After the Rain*

After the Rain (figure 61) This panel was a development of *Harvest*, but in this case the dull blue linen used as background was mounted on a stretcher and a warp was made with *Sylko Perlé*. Strips of different blues, turquoise and lime greens were irregularly darned into this warp, and some pieces of green glass tubing were suspended at intervals.

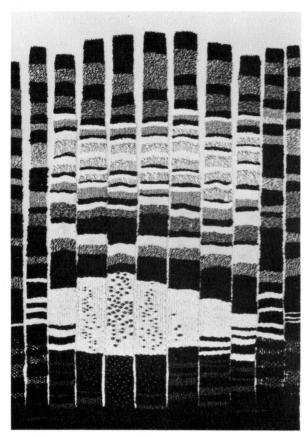

62 *Fossil Strata* by Eleanor Scarfe, 1219 mm × 1016 mm (48 in. × 40 in.). Strips woven in white and textured black and white threads incorporating black beads are attached to a white linen ground

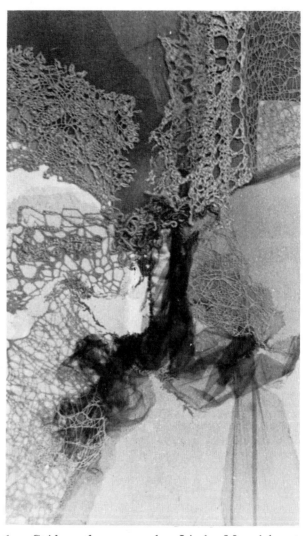

63 *Spiders Anonymous* by Linda Mosedale at Manchester College of Art and Design. Crochet and knitting in slubbed and fine wool on woollen background, with blanket stitch on wire, and bullion knots. Subtle tints of light browns, dull pinks and greys (some moving to purple) are used

64   *Sea-Fret*, 914 mm × 533 mm (36 in. × 21 in.).
Coarsely woven white nylon fabric (some warp and
weft threads withdrawn), stretched over a blue–
green background on which is sewn a large yellowish
green sun with long threads of darker blues and
greens below it. Exhibited in the Ascher Award
Exhibition

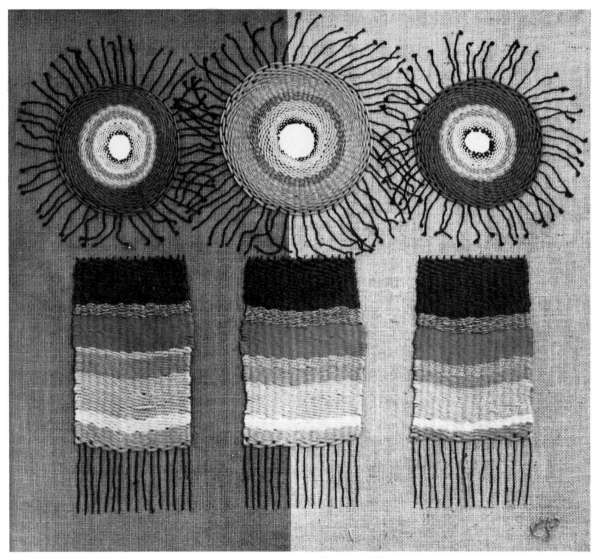

65 *Trio* by Eleanor Scarfe, 610 mm × 660 mm (24 in. × 26 in.). Shapes in brilliant red, green, blue, yellow and pink are woven on a black warp and attached to a background of red and yellow hessian

Patchwork

For patchwork panels, of the type illustrated on plate 5, a line drawing exactly like the finished panel must first be made on paper, heavyweight *Vilene* or hardboard. This is then cut into sections along the lines, and the pieces are covered with fabric, the turnings being glued or sewn down on the wrong side, so that the stitches do not come through. The sections are then fitted into place and sewn together or glued to a base.

In *Variabilis*, figure 66, the sections are cut out from a paper pattern, but the paper was discarded and the pieces machined into place.

The background of *Platform*, plate 4, is a patchwork of tweeds, hessian and cotton. The strips in the foreground are of felt.

In *Stripes and Spots*, figure 67, some of the shapes are constructed so that they slope upwards from the surface and *Flower Piece,* figure 68, shows the use of a patterned background.

In *Square and Circles,* figure 69, the squares are made separately using different materials (including ric-rac braid, beads and felt), and different treatments. They are mounted on card and fixed to a firm background. This is a successful use of the three primary colours, and a project of this type could be used for co-operative work.

Plate 5
Tension by Alice Timmins

57

66   *Variabilis* by Alice Timmins

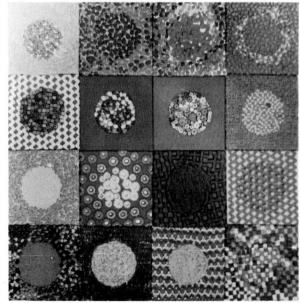

67 *Stripes and Spots* Panel in red, white and blue by Pat Clarke, Manchester Polytechnic, School of Embroidery

68 *Flower Piece* by Eirian Short

69 *Squares and Circles* by Ann Gow, third year student at Manchester Polytechnic, School of Embroidery

In figure 70 *Vilene* is used for patterns, which are cut from a 50 mm (2 in.) side diamond template. As the patterns are to be left in, the fabric patches are tacked over them so that no stitches show on the right side.

The patches at the top and bottom of the panel must be very neatly finished, and the turnings at the top should be folded so that they are not visible (figure 71). The edges are sewn neatly to the *Vilene*. Each of these patches is backed

70   Patchwork panel by Alice Timmins

with a similar patch (wrong sides together) and the two are caught together with several stitches over each other at the top points.

The bottom halves of the back patches are hemmed down over the lining of the panel (figure 72).

A length of brass pelmet strip, obtainable at hardware or some chain stores, is passed between the top patches.

This type of hanging can be used with any shape of patch.

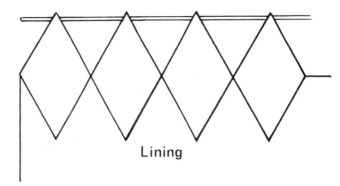

Lining

72

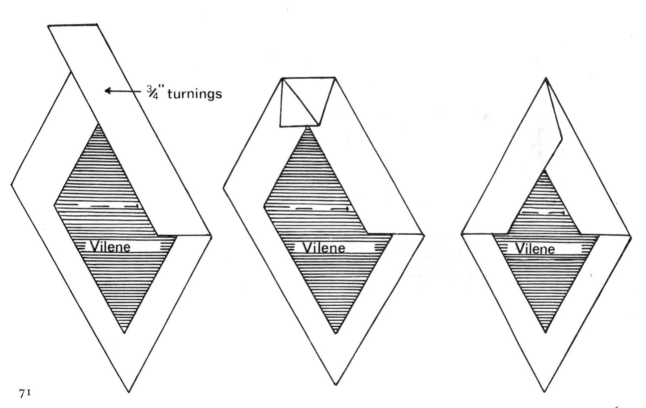

¾" turnings

Vilene

Vilene

Vilene

71

Fabric strips

Strips of fabric may be used in many ways.

In *Unseeing Eyes*, figure 73, they are sewn in place with brown mercerised machine cotton using herringbone, feather stitch and straight stitch. Browns, orange and pinks are used with touches of dark blues and reds. The lighter tones are grouped together to form the face.

The long strips used in *Midnight Sun*, plate 6, are torn, and the frayed edges contribute to the desired effect.

In the two samples (figures 74 and 75) some of the strips of fabric are tufted on rug canvas and some are machined down. Some coarse cross stitch and darned stitches are carried out in rug wool.

In *Summer's Day*, plate 8, strips of fabric are used for straight and running stitches, tufting and threading.

73 *Unseeing Eyes,* 457 mm × 381 mm (18 in. × 15 in.)

74 Sampler by Ann Gow, Manchester Polytechnic, School of Embroidery

75 Sampler by Ann Gow, Manchester Polytechnic, School of Embroidery

Plate 6
Midnight Sun by Alice Timmins

In the possession of Mr and Mrs Grenfell Baines

Machine and hand stitchery

Although embroidery may be superfluous on some fabric hangings, others may need some areas of stitchery to add texture or decoration, or to emphasize a particular statement. Some may consist entirely of machine or hand embroidery on a background of fabric or some interesting material.

Many of the threads used in traditional work are no longer available, and this fact, combined with new experimental attitudes towards embroidery, have led to the use of unconventional materials in their place. Stitchery with string, ribbon, unravelled threads, knitting wool, lurex, wire, raffia and cut or torn strips of fabric can show great vitality.

Traditional techniques may be used in unexpected and exciting ways. Stitches may be worked one over the other, and long stitches, impractical for most purposes, may be used freely for panels (figures 22, 23, 24 and 87). Not only can interesting linear effects be obtained, but shapes may be filled in entirely with stitchery (figure 78).

Much experimental work can be done using the sewing machine; the quickness of execution is well suited to the speed of life today.

76 *Doodling,* 457 mm × 178 mm (18 in. × 7 in.) by Rachel Campbell

77 *Drought*, 559 mm × 330 mm (22 in. × 13 in.).
Made on sacking and embroidered chiefly with
string salvaged from parcels

78 *Princess*, Two simple shapes machined to a darker blue background and covered with rows of stitchery in threads of different types including thin strips of knitted nylon. (See also figure 80)

Page 68
79 *Revert,* 762 mm × 914 mm (30 in. × 36 in.) by Anne Butler. Orange background, blue hessian applied, and on that a square placed diagonally. In the centre of this, lace is applied with ribbon worked on top, and around this herringbone stitch in different threads including ribbon. Squares in white felt, are added

81　*Towers,* 1830 mm × 1067 mm (6 ft × 3½ ft)
by Alice Timmins. Grey 'towers' with brown, green
or dark blue bases. Machine stitchery, washers,
metal rings, jet beads and a little hand stitchery
were added. Each section was worked separately.

Suitable for co-operative work. Purchased for
Edgehill College of Education, Ormskirk, Lancashire

80　*Tower,* 457 mm (18 in.) long, 95 mm (3¾ in.)
at base, tapering to 82 mm (3¼ in.) at top. Black
embroidery by hand and machine on a white
ground. Pattern discs are used. Polystyrene circles
are slices from the middle of a purchase recording
roll from a supermarket

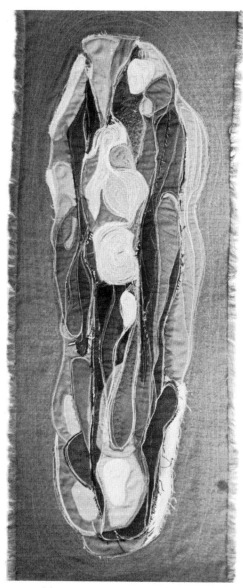

82a *Driftwood*

82b *Driftwood,* 1219 mm × 406 mm (48 in. × 16 in.). Based on a piece of wood picked up on the seashore. Browns, from very pale to very dark, are sewn by machine to a blue–green background. Some transparent fabrics are used, and some hand embroidery is added.

70

83 *War and Peace* by Thea Gregoor of Holland.
Photograph by courtesy of the Stedelijk Museum,
Amsterdam

84   Panel by Kryn Giezen, Holland.
Photograph by courtesy of the
Stedelijk Museum, Amsterdam

Plate 7
Desert Island Disc by Alice Timmins

Folded and rolled fabric

This series of panels had its origin in an 'import' load of timber spars on Bristol docks. The best way of representing them seemed to be 'whirls' made as in figures 88 and 89, using rough fabrics (striped hessian and coarse linen) which suggested the texture of the wood. They were fastened together with thick hairy brown string, knotted and passed through holes drilled in the two strips of wood.

Desert Island Disc, plate 7, in various shades of yellow, turquoise, royal blue, olive green and soft brown—was made in much the same way as *Import*, figure 90*b*. The strips of fabric were folded twice or several times, tacked, and then stuck together instead of being sewn. All raw edges were at the back, and the disc was stuck to a foundation of plywood.

For *Tree*, figure 91, the fabric strips were cut on the bias (about 25 mm (1 in.) wide) and were rolled and sewn down so that the raw edges were hidden. Some strips of shiny rayon furnishing fabric with one edge frayed were sewn on.

Burning Bush, figure 92, was made from rectangles of fabric rolled into cornet shapes and sewn down. Long straight stitches and a few detached chain stitches were added.

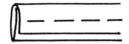

85

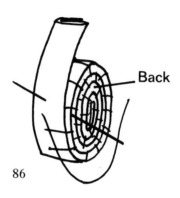

Back

86

73

87*a*   Inspiration for *Import*

87*b*   *Import*, 406 mm × 356 mm (16 in. × 14 in.)

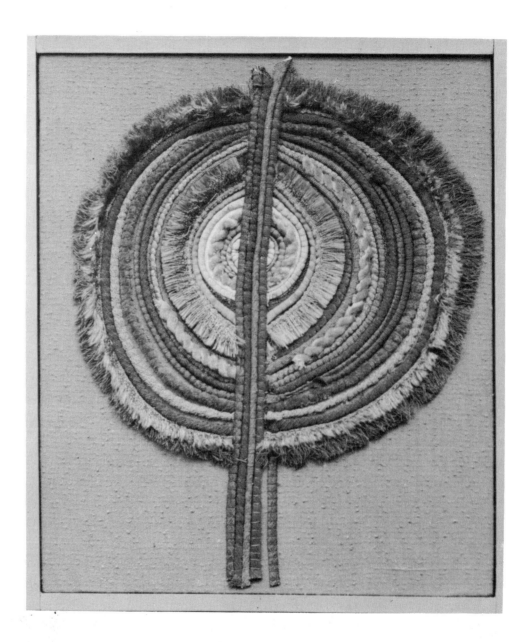

88 *Tree,* 406 mm × 356 mm (16 in. × 14 in.)

89 *Burning Bush*, 154 mm × 229 mm (10 in. ×
9 in.). Brilliant reds, yellows, orange pink and
magneta with dark red stitchery

Collage

In the strictest sense, a collage is a piece of work in which all the materials are glued down. When fabric is used, however, stitches seem to be a sensible way of securing some of the materials to it, and in most fabric collages stitchery is to be found.

All kinds of things can be used in a collage; waste or discarded materials, (lollypop sticks, used matches, tin cans, old garments, etc) 'found' objects (such as pieces of bark, driftwood, stones, and glass), or any natural or manufactured object which will help to carry out the theme.

90 *Lords and Lady of the Woodlands* by Josephine Olivia Harrison. A true collage as all the materials—net, chiffon, feathers, wool, satin velvet and wire spirals—are stuck down. Brown, soft greens, orange and salmon pinks are used with brilliant greens on a dull turquoise background

91

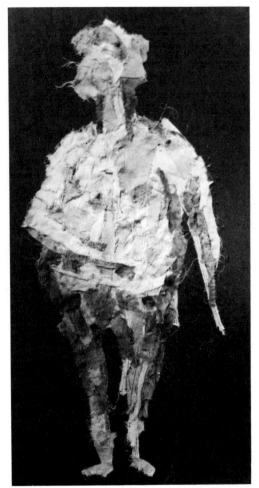

92

91   *Monkeys* by Margaret Kaye

92   *Figure* by Margaret Kaye

93 *Number* **1**. Appliqué and stitchery panel by Nik Krevitsky, USA

94   *Tanque Verde Ranch* by Bucky King, USA

Plate 8
Summer's Day by Marjorie Timmins

95   *Owl* by Henrietta Shuttleworth, USA

Suppliers in Great Britain

Background fabrics, threads and all embroidery accessories

Mrs Mary Allen
Turnditch, Derbyshire

Art Needlework Industries Ltd
7 St Michael's Mansions
Ship Street, Oxford

I. M. Jervie
21–3 West Port
Arbroath, Angus, Scotland

Ladies Work Society
138 Brompton Road
London SW3

John Lewis
Oxford Street
London W1

The Needlewoman Shop
146 Regent Street
London W1

Mace and Nairn
89 Crane Street
Salisbury, Wiltshire

Nottingham Handicraft Company
Melton Road
West Bridgford, Nottingham

Mrs Joan Trickett
110 Marsden Road
Burnley, Lancashire

Betty Veal
Waterloo Buildings
London Road
Southampton, Hampshire

Watts and Co Ltd
7 Tufton Street
London SW1

Felt and hessian

The Felt and Hessian Shop
34 Greville Street
London EC1

Longmeadow Felt Company Ltd
PO Box 5
Kidderminster, Worcestershire

Metal threads

Louis Grossé Ltd
36 Manchester Street
London W1

Bernina Service
3 Burton's Arcade
Leeds 1, Yorkshire

String

Mister Bosun's Locker
East Street
Chichester, Sussex

All yacht chandlers and stationers

Templates for patchwork

J.E.M. Patchwork Template Company
Pyrton,
Watlington, Oxfordshire

A. M. Row & Son Ltd
42 Market Place,
Ripon, Yorkshire

The Needlewoman Shop,
146 Regent Street
London W1

Polystyrene

General stores and Do-it-Yourself shops

Adhesives

Copydex and *Evostick*
Most stationers and general stores

Marvin Medium
Margros Ltd
Monument House
Monument Way West
Woking, Surrey

Suppliers in USA

Threads, wools and embroidery accessories

American Crewel Studio
Box 553 Westfield
New Jersey 07091

American Thread Corporation
90 Park Avenue
New York, NY

Bucky King
Embroideries Unlimited
121 South Drive
Pittsburgh
Pennsylvania 15238

Tinsel Trading Company
7 West 36 Street
New York 18, NY

Yarn Bazaar
Yarncrafts Limited
3146 M Street
North West Washington, DC

Crewel and tapestry wool

Appleton Brothers of London
West Main Road
Little Compton
Rhode Island 02837

Adhesives

Sobo and *Elmer's Glue*
Hardward stores, most general stores and
builder's supply houses

Templates (also known as *stencils*)

Art material supply stores

Bibliography

Creative Play with Fabric and Threads Jean Carter, B. T. Batsford Ltd, London and Taplinger Publications, New York

Simple Stitches Anne Butler, B. T. Batsford Ltd, London and Frederick A. Praeger, New York

Stitchery: Art and Craft Nik Krevitsky, Reinhold Publishing Corporation, New York

Dictionary of Embroidery Stitches Mary Thomas, Hodder & Stoughton, London and William Morrow & Co. Inc., New York

Your Machine Embroidery Dorothy Benson, Sylvan Press, London

Introducing Patchwork Alice Timmins, B. T. Batsford Ltd, London and Watson-Guptill Publications, New York

Decorative Wall Hangings David van Dommeleu, Vane Publishers, Kaye & Ward, London

You are an Artist Fred Gettings, Paul Hamlyn, Feltham, Middlesex

The Golden Pleasure Book of Art Fred Gettings, Paul Hamlyn, Feltham, Middlesex

The Critical Eye Guido Ballo, Heinemann Ltd, London

Basic Design: the dynamics of Visual Form Maurice de Sausmarez, Studio Vista, London and Reinhold Publishing Corporation, New York

Paul Klee on Modern Art Faber & Faber, London

Life under the Microscope Jíroveč, Boucek and Fiala, Spring Books, Paul Hamlyn, Feltham, Middlesex

Precious Stones and other Crystals R. Melz, Thames & Hudson, London

Index